Unit 7

The Animal Kingdom

Mc
Graw
Hill
Education

Contents

Sun Fun

See the duck.
Duck can go up.

Pup is fun.
A pup can run.

Cat can nap.
A cat can lick it.

Cub is fit.

A cub can run in the sun.

Kid can have fun.
A kid can hop for fun.

6

Pup and Cub

I am Pup.
I can get in mud.

I am Cub.
I can go up.

Pup can not run up it.
Pup can run in the sun.

Can Cub get in the hut?
Can Pup get in the cup?

Pup and Cub run a lot.
Pup and Cub have fun.

Wet Gus

Gus is my pet pup.
Gus can wag for fun.

Gus can tug on it.
Can Gus win?

Gus can win it!
Gus got mud on a leg.

It is a lot of mud.
I can get Gus wet.

Mom and Dad pat Gus.
They like Gus.

See a Bug?

See a bug on a big log?
It can get wet.

(bkgd) ursula1OO/iStock/Getty Images, (bl) skynetphoto/ iStock/Getty Images, (tr) Cre8tive Studios/Alamy

Red bug and big bug dig.
They can dig in mud.

The red bug can sit.
It got on top of a pig!

A big bug can hop up.
Get up big bug!

23

See a big wet web?
A bug can not win in it!

24

Rex the Vet

Rex is a vet.
Rex can get in the van.

"I want in," said Rex.
Rex had to fix the fox.

Rex can fix the sick fox.
Rex set it in a big box.

Rex can tag a red fox.
Rex can tag a big ox.

Rex can get in the van.
Rex can get to a lab.

Fox Had a Big Box

Fox had a big box.
Sad Ox sat on the box.

"Fix it!" said mad Fox.
"I want to," said sad Ox.

Ox can cut six with an ax.
Fox can mix it.

Ox hit Fox on the leg.
It is red and big.

They get in the tan van.
Vick Vet can fix it up!

DECODABLE WORDS
Target Phonics Elements
  Initial and Medial *u*: up, cub, duck, fun, pup, run, sun

HIGH-FREQUENCY WORDS
for, have
Review: a, go, is, see, the

Pup and Cub WORD COUNT: 53

DECODABLE WORDS
Target Phonics Elements
  Initial and Medial *u*: up, cub, cup, fun, hut, mud, pup, run

HIGH-FREQUENCY WORDS
have
Review: a, and, go, I, the

DECODABLE WORDS
Target Phonics Elements
  Initial and Final *g*, Initial *w*; *g*: get, got, Gus, leg, tug; *w*: wag, wet, win

HIGH-FREQUENCY WORDS
of, they
Review: a, and, for, like, I, is, my

See a Bug? WORD COUNT: 59

DECODABLE WORDS
Target Phonics Elements
  Initial and Final *g*, Initial *w*; *g*: get, got, big, bug, dig, log, pig; *w*: web, wet, win

HIGH-FREQUENCY WORDS
of, they
Review: a, see, the

DECODABLE WORDS
Target Phonics Elements
  Initial *v*, Final *x*; *v*: van, vet; *x*: box, fix, fox, ox, Rex, six

HIGH-FREQUENCY WORDS
said, want
Review: a, I, is, the, to

Fox Had a Big Box WORD COUNT: 61

DECODABLE WORDS
Target Phonics Elements
  Initial *v*, Final *x*; *v*: van, vet, Vick; *x*: ax, box, fix, fox, mix, ox, six

HIGH-FREQUENCY WORDS
said, want
Review: a, an, and, I, is, the, they, to, with

37

HIGH-FREQUENCY WORDS TAUGHT TO DATE

Grade K

a
and
are
can
do
for
go
have
he
I
is
like
little
my
of
said
see
she
the
they
to
want
was
we
with
you

DECODING SKILLS TAUGHT TO DATE
Initial and final consonant *m*; short *a*; initial *s*; initial and final consonant *p*; initial and final consonant *t*; initial and medial vowel *i*; initial and final consonant *n*; initial *c*; initial and medial vowel *o*; initial and final *d*; initial consonant *h*; initial and medial vowel *e*; initial consonants *f* and *r*; initial and final consonant *b*; initial consonant *l*; initial consonant *k*; final digraph *ck*; initial and medial vowel *u*; initial and final *g*; initial *w*; final consonant *x*; initial consonant *v*